Fun With Nuns

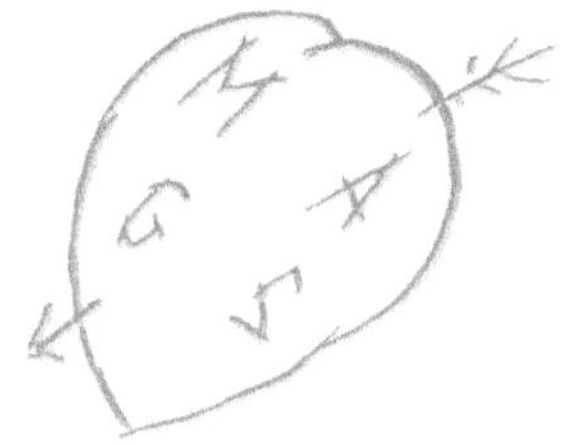

Fun With Nuns

...and Other **HORROR** Stories

A. J. Caliendo

Illustrated by

Sidney Wuenschell

SANGWICH PRESS

ISBN (paperback): 979-8-9912139-0-5
ISBN (ebook): 979-8-9912139-1-2

For Stephen, Sonny, Marley,
Amelia, Gianni, and Stella

"Love is how you stay alive,
even after you are gone."

MITCH ALBOM

Contents

Chapter 1

waiting ... and waiting ...
and waiting

PATIENCE IS NOT one of my precious few virtues.

I'm that guy! The one who sits at traffic lights with white knuckles and gritted teeth, cursing every wasted second that I could have used to take a nap. (My wife tells friends that I get a serious case of Tourette's syndrome every time I get behind the wheel.) And it doesn't matter whether I'm in a hurry. If I want to sit, I'll do it in my overstuffed La-Z-Boy with the heated, vibrating seat in front of a football game with a beer in one hand and the remote in the other. If I'm in a car, I want it to be moving, damn it.

I'm also the guy who will stomp out of a doctor's or dentist's office if I'm still in the waiting room more than ten minutes past my appointment time. Sitting on cold, hard faux leather while avoiding eye contact with a sniffling, sneezing middle-aged woman with orange streaks in her hair and a golf ball–sized cough drop in her mouth, who for some reason is just dying to tell a total stranger about her ailments, her freakishly accomplished children, her intolerable husband, and how much I look like her cousin Ernie who is doing two to five upstate for armed robbery, is not my idea of the perfect way to while away a spring afternoon. Instead, I give the receptionist my phone number and tell her to have the doctor call me when he's ready, and I'll see if I can squeeze him in.

I badger the guy at the quick-change oil place to find me a ride home and come and pick me up when my car is done—fifteen minutes later. I race little old ladies to the checkout line, so I don't have to wait for them to gape at the checker while she scans the food and then, only after the order has been bagged and the total announced, decides to count out the correct change or begin writing a check while I watch the seasons change. (Actually, I've been noticing this one is getting tougher. Now that the age gap is closing, the old girls beat me to the counter as often as not.)

So it was, on a gloomy, drizzling October day, my patience was taxed to the limit as I sat behind the wheel of my 1980 Toyota Corolla in the final year of the bygone millennium and waited for my tardy passenger. It didn't help that the crumbling, tree-lined street could possibly be the loneliest, most depressing location on the planet. The scenery that stretched out before me was a mind-numbing combination of gray sky, raindrops that dotted my windshield waiting for the swipe of the wiper blades to whisk them away, and piles of leaves that two weeks earlier had no doubt hung on the trees in the brilliant, flaming reds, yellows, and oranges of early autumn. They were now lying in large clumps, brown and sodden on the pavement below.

But I had to admit that the weather wasn't the sole, or even the main, cause of my increasingly foul mood that threatened to sabotage the happy face I wanted to put on for this mini-reunion that I both welcomed and dreaded. That blame had to be placed on a laundry list of fears that crept through my mind, defying the attempts I made to exorcise them with sight, sound, and lingering daydreams about Sophia Loren, which I was being told by the ghosts of the army of nuns that haunted my early years, were "impure" and needed to be confessed to Father McClatchy in the little box of horrors on Saturday. Much more on that subject later.

I recalled both fondly and angrily, this was by no means unusual for my friend of forty years. Many times I had stood on the corner of Elm and McGarrity, which was a full block from his house, my knee jiggling while I waited, and wondered why my buddy couldn't seem to be on time even for an afternoon of sheer pleasure at the Eastwood Theater to see a double feature and cartoons. It seemed to me at the time that if he would let me come to meet him at his house, I could light a fire under him so we could get there early enough to hit the concession stand for popcorn and candy and still get inside to see the coming attractions.

Since I had not passed a gas station, store, or diner during the last fifteen miles of two-and-a-half-hour trip, I pushed the thought of driving back for another coffee out of my mind. It was no pleasure having to walk through the dripping trees on soppy ground to expunge the two cups I had on the way up. I had no desire to do it again, not to mention the risk of my buddy coming out to an empty street in my absence.

I cursed my now-evaporated willpower that kept me from reaching for a pack of Kools on the counter display where I had purchased my first cup of java. Two hundred seventeen days was a long time to go without smoke, only to blow it now, but on this occasion, I thought I would have been justified in breaking the streak.

So my mood was growing more sour and anxious as I tapped my fingers on the steering wheel, fiddled with the radio, and noted that I had long since "outgrown" the compact coupe that I had kept running on chewing gum and gum bands for the past year. "Why take on another car payment?" I would rationalize as I squeezed my extra forty pounds into the driver's seat while trying to ignore the fact that the money I saved on buying a car that better fit my burgeoning bulk would reward me by ending a four-year epidemic of leg cramps and chronic bus butt, not to mention a mountain of chiropractor bills.

To add to the misery, I had, as is my habit in all scheduled engagements, arrived more than thirty minutes early for this enigmatic rendezvous. I was now taking out my aggressions on the old car by pounding out the drum solo in the old song "Wipeout" on the steering wheel as my grief and aggravation crawled toward the hour mark.

But on this day, the worst part of waiting was the additional burden of uncertainty about the prospect of facing my friend after not seeing him for so long. The questions running through my head haunted and worried me. Would he still be the same guy I knew? I doubted that. Surely the experiences of the past thirty years would have had some effect on his development. I noted all the changes in my personality, demeanor and philosophy over that time. Maturity didn't seem to fit into that list of changes, thank God, and I had to assume that my friend would not be immune to that same metamorphosis.

Would he immediately notice those changes in me? Certainly the extra girth and the addition of the graying beard that I had worn for the past three years would take a little time for him to get used to, but what about the cynicism that had replaced the devil-may-care ambivalence of my youth? What of my disdain for the self-absorbed hedonists that had replaced the idealistic, "we-must-save-the-world" hedonists of our formative years?

Would we find enough to talk about to fill the two-and-a-half-hour trip back through some of the gloomiest, unmitigatedly boring terrain I had ever crossed?

I didn't want to wait any longer for those answers. I wanted to confront them now and make whatever stupid blunders the fates had in store for me on this inauspicious occasion and to find out if this reunion was motivated only by my old friend's need of a ride or by a genuine desire to renew the camaraderie we once shared.

By this time, I had been sitting and waiting for thirty-five minutes, plus the thirty-minute early time. I had already finished the *New York Times* crossword puzzle—the Monday edition, which I usually shun as an insult to my superior solving abilities—and read everything in the morning paper that that didn't contain information about gala parties where tuxedoed men with razor-cut hair (real or implanted) and gowned and bejeweled women smiled reluctantly for the photographer, who was there to record their selfless big-dollar donations to save the damned baby seals at an affair that cost enough to feed the hungry children of our city for a year.

The only radio station I could pull in with a minimum of static played country and western music and featured a jolly team of drawlers who I think were named Lum and Abner, but I might have made that up. These Elwoods had gotten on my nerves thirty-four minutes earlier, so I started to daydream about them in their bib overalls, with their eight collective teeth. But I dreaded the thought of a third listening to the only cassette tape I had the foresight to bring with me, The Faces' "A Nod Is as Good as a Wink." Buck Owens and Roy Clark a-pickin'-and-a grinnin' and Dolly Parton—okay, I like Dolly Parton. Okay—I *love* Dolly Parton. Tapping my fingers to the music seemed even less amusing than usual on this chilly, dank, and foggy fall day, when even the few remaining colorful leaves that clung stubbornly to the maple and sycamore trees, in this land of natural beauty and manmade ugliness, seemed strangely depressing.

Adding to my deprivation-induced self-pity was the fact that I never wanted a cigarette as badly as I did at this moment and, like at the coffee shop, I again cursed the willpower that "saved" me from the temptation of cigarettes out of the greasy spoon where I stopped off for my first coffee, undercooked bacon and scrambled eggs so runny I had to eat them with a spoon. At the time, I convinced myself that my record fourteen months, four days of abstinence were worth salvaging. Now, sitting alone in gloomy silence in the back of beyond on the most miserable day God could muster outside of Transylvania, lung cancer seemed like a small price to pay to satisfy my oral fixation.

All of those sensory deprivations, I realized to my horror, left me alone with my thoughts, a dangerous partnership for one who has been preparing for days to be completely spontaneous and nonchalant when the moment arrived. It gave me more time than I wanted or needed to reflect on all that had happened in the years since I began the longest-lasting, happiest, saddest, most fulfilling, and most frustrating relationship of my life.

Chapter 2

Billy

BILLY TILDON and I became friends in the fourth grade as I started another year of being scared spitless to speak to a new kid, lest I say something offensive—my stock-in-trade—and get a good butt whoopin' not administered by my father. I learned about the dangers of misspeaking to the nuns from my older brother Gino's horror stories of his numerous run-ins with the woman in black. Billy must have just intuited the Machiavellian sensibilities that lie under those hot wool habits with the white wimples covering the head area like a hoodie. He had been "public" for his first three years of education.

He told me that his new stepmother had insisted on the switch to teach him respect and discipline. His father had offered no resistance to his new wife's demand. Later that year, he made the teary-eyed confession, "I miss my mother so bad." I quickly looked away from him to preserve my cool.

Billy's sweet demeanor, plus the fact that his last name didn't end in a vowel, gave him a distinct advantage with the redneck Kentucky nuns, but a big disadvantage with the other kids whose names did. In a Pittsburgh suburb with a *paisan* on every corner, that was tantamount to a mortal sin. We could even put a buck down on the number—no lottery then—on the playground at recess. To this day, I still put my money down with the bookie. It's more fun.

It was 1960, and it looked like we were about to elect John Fitzgerald Kennedy our first Roman Catholic president. The nuns informed us in no uncertain terms that if we didn't pray for the handsome, dashing, charismatic, great-hair papist's victory over the monkey-faced, sweaty-lipped Richard M. Nixon, we would go to hell, go directly to hell, and wouldn't even pass Go and collect $200.

So it was that JFK was elected the thirty-fifth president of the United States. I've always wondered how the "penguins" felt when, years after his assassination in 1963, he was revealed to be a philanderer with a crook for a father. That thought always made me smile.

Billy had no brothers or sisters, and I was the product of an accidental pregnancy, a fact of which I was reminded throughout my childhood and adolescence every time I screwed up or asked for money. My only sibling was my aforementioned brother, eight years my senior, who, until he mercifully moved out of the house at nineteen after getting Angela Bellini pregnant, put all his time and energy into trying to regain his status as an only child. I slept with one eye open the first eleven years of my life.

So, neither Billy nor I had any idea whether people about our own age and approximate size were any less of a threat than my father, who would give my brother and me the old dago backhand if we dared ask for so much as a glass of water while visiting relatives.

From the beginning, we were an odd pair, my new friend and I. I was big for my age, kind of a featherless Baby Huey, and Billy was a runt, barely coming up to my shoulders when he stood on tiptoe to whisper something in my ear that he was afraid to let anyone else hear.

He was smart, something that was evident from the first day he was at Holy Cross school, because he was able to answer several questions the teacher put to the class to see if we were awake and relatively free of brain damage from asking for water while visiting relatives.

I, on the other hand, had no interest in improving my intellect beyond my uncanny ability to memorize dialogue from *The Howdy Doody Show* and *Captain Midnight* after only one viewing. That particular aspect of my personality earned me a reputation that followed me through high school and beyond, which prompted me to write my own epitaph as a young man. "He wasn't stupid, he was just lazy," my tombstone will read, followed by, "And does everything have to be a joke to him?", an accusation constantly leveled by parents, teachers, and other adults, to which I replied, "Yes, or I would be forced to kill you!" But that turned out to be a blessing, not a curse, because I started out my career writing a humor column for a dinky newspaper, which ended up being syndicated around the country.

✝

And that was probably the biggest difference between my new friend and me. His method of coping with fear of the unknown was to hide behind a shy façade and timid demeanor, a character trait that would change a bit as he got older. When I was faced with a frightening situation, I did my best to talk and joke my way out of it, which got me out of a lot of scrapes, not because of my natural charm, but because I was too annoying for most people, kids and adults alike, to deal with.

So it was that our differences brought us together. I admired his intelligence (I disagreed with the adults; I was *sure* I was stupid) and his ability to talk only when he had something to say. At first, he thought my size would help him through any physical encounters with the bullies we had both been warned to avoid. That was until he found out that I was a bigger sissy than he was. After that he became fascinated with my tendency to get out of trouble by making a complete fool of myself. It was a match made, if not in heaven, then at least in purgatory or limbo, which is now closed. More about that later.

To this point, I have neglected to mention that my friend and I attended a Catholic or, as my parents, who often mispronounced single-syllable words and occasionally each other's names, would call "para-ocular" school, called Our Lady of the Holy Cross. Our fourth-grade teacher, no doubt selected because she was young and hadn't yet developed the proper wrist action to administer a good ruler slap to older kids who were capable of committing bigger sins, was Sister Mary Immaculata.

The good (comparatively speaking) Sister took an instant fancy to Billy, a rare thing between a nun and a boy in those days. Nuns were taught in convent school that the Y chromosome was the source of all the evil in the world and all males are to be looked upon as a blight on the earth that should be completely wiped out if at all possible. I suppose it never occurred to them that if they succeeded in their efforts, there would be no more children to torture, and they would all be out of a job.

Exceptions, or indulgences as the church called them, to the man-as-Satan philosophy were given to the men of the parish who were willing to waste an entire Saturday afternoon hauling nuns all over the place because they were forbidden, by some rule handed down from Jesus Christ himself, to ever drive a car. Some years later, the Son of God rescinded that law, and the men of Catholic parishes all over the country were able to sit down in peace and watch college football once more.

But Sister Immaculata obviously saw something in Billy that made her care. Maybe it was his obvious vulnerability, or maybe some foreboding of a troubled life to come, that made people and nuns alike want to take him under their wings, but the feeling was definitely there in our fourth-grade teacher. I've got to confess that, although I wasn't conscious of it at the time, that is also part of what drew me to the little guy with the shy smile and the sad eyes. In hindsight I understand that it was those eyes, as crystal blue as a husky puppy's and as soul-piercing as a fiery sermon from a tent preacher, that truly fueled my, and others', fascination with this gentle boy.

Uncharacteristically, Billy had made the first gesture toward friendship on that third day of school. I think he would have done it sooner, but there was no recess for us the first two school days because of rain, and we rode different school buses to and from Holy Cross. Those are about the only two opportunities Catholic school children had to interact in those days because, as we learned during our first moment there, *the* most terrible sin of all was the sin of talking in the classroom, the lunchroom, the bathroom, the library, the hallways, church, in front of the school while waiting for the bus, or any other place where the sound of our voices would reach the ears of the holiest of holies in the long, black dresses. That rule doomed me to hell almost before my little six-year-old butt hit the chair for the first time.

Day three was a sunny one, so just after lunch—during which I was threatened with expulsion from school and excommunication from the Catholic Church for trying to negotiate the trade of a peanut butter sandwich for a tuna—we were allowed to go outside for fifteen minutes to play kickball. My friend, emboldened by the temporary suspension of our imposed vow of silence, approached me while we were waiting for our turns.

"My name is Billy," he said, extending his hand in a way that made me think he must have picked up the gesture from watching Ward Cleaver on *Leave It to Beaver*.

I was so stunned that I couldn't even think of a wisecrack. "I'm Enzo," I muttered, looking down on this funny little guy with a crooked smile and a gully-sized gap between his front teeth. "Where d'ya live?"

"In Brightwood," he answered, naming a part of town that was just a little swankier than the middle-class neighborhood where I lived. "How about you?"

"Claremont, "I said, adding for no particular reason other than a ten-year-old's version of trying to keep up with the Joneses, "But we've been thinking about moving to Brightwood as soon as my dad gets this big inheritance from his great-aunt and we get rich."

"That would be neat," he replied, probably thinking he had already committed a major blunder by speaking to this lunatic in the first place. But I guess he must have figured that since he was in this far, he might as well go all the way.

"I think you're funny and I'd like to be your friend," he finally spit out.

Quickly regaining my penchant for the snappy retort, I said, "Yeah, sure, okay."

Making it even stranger that I was so willing to accept Billy as my first real friend—not counting Gina, my baby-sitter, who told me we were friends when she wanted me to keep my mouth shut about sneaking her boyfriend into the house—is the fact that, unlike most of us at Holy Cross, this kid had light hair and even lighter skin. In Our Lady of the Holy Cross parish, not being of Italian descent was almost as weird as not being Catholic. Worse yet, Billy's parents didn't fit the mold of any of the other ethnic groups that the anything-but-silent majority could readily identify and insult.

But what I remember most about that third day of school is that it turned out to be a significant event in my life. It is a day for which I will always be grateful, even though it would later be the cause of no small amount of sadness, regret, frustration, and fear in my life. Still, if I had it to do over, I wouldn't hesitate a second.

For a long while, I didn't know what a deeply complicated individual I had befriended. Billy clearly had secrets that he wanted to keep hidden. I was no stranger to being shut out of information, and it never sat well with me. "You're in this country now; you speak English!" my mean little grandfather would say, less out of a desire to assure my complete assimilation for my benefit, I knew, and more to keep the juiciest tidbits of family gossip secret out of spite. Relatives would often lapse into Italian, knowing my understanding of the language—and that of my cousins—was on a par with the McGintys next door. (Although my accent was spot-on.) Non-Italian spouses in the family, including a beloved aunt, received the same exclusionary treatment. Oh, did I mention the oilcloth-wrapped gun I found in the closet that time, that may or may not have played a role in my grandfather's emigration? Good, I hoped not. It's a secret. But to return to the point, when Billy began to open up, it was only because he could no longer hide the obvious from a straightforward extrovert, who had no problem ignoring the signals "I don't want to talk about it," or "It's none of your business," or even the times he came straight out and said the words. Even after Billy let me into his other world, I had to swear to never tell another human being about this inner sanctum he had erected for himself. As it ended up, I would one day tell my father some of what he had told me. By then it no longer mattered.

It was then I began to understand a little of what was going on behind those husky-puppy eyes, kind but piercing; urgent, like an SOS was being telegraphed from their depths. I could never square his circumstance with the God the nuns were forever telling us was kind and loving—I wondered if He could have had it in for my kind, fragile friend—as if he were being punished for some grievous sin that he committed without knowing. And the saddest part was that William Raymond Tildon, innocent and hopeful as he was, seemed to wonder that too.

Chapter 3

Teddy Manfredi

As the late summer gave way to fall and school was becoming more routine, if no less life-threatening, Billy and I began to expand our circle of friends. Unlike a lot of best friends, there was no jealousy between us when we met new kids and invited them into our lives. We just seemed to know instinctively that what we had couldn't be shared by anyone else, only observed at close range.

The first kid we welcomed into our tight little circle was not among the first hundred or so individuals that I would have picked if I had thought about such things back then. The circumstances under which he joined us were stranger still.

Theodore "Teddy" Manfredi, another transfer from public school, was a kid whose parents should have just named him "Beat me up and give me a wedgie" and been done with it. Besides the rhyming name, which kids pick up on faster than a bum pounces on a twenty-dollar bill in the street, Teddy was obviously never homeschooled in the art of ten-year-old cool. Even I had gotten a few tips in that area between pummelings from my sadistic brother, who didn't want to be embarrassed if anyone made the connection, because no matter how much he beat on me, I refused to change my last name.

Also unfortunate was the fact that Teddy had serious allergies and a nonstop runny nose that made him an undesirable associate, especially at the lunch table. He was round faced with blotchy red skin that made him look like a ten-year-old drunkard, a nose that he wouldn't grow into until after high school, and bloodshot eyes that not only enhanced the drunk look but itched so bad from his allergies that he constantly rubbed them, giving the impression that he was always crying.

Teddy's dad was what my mean little grandfather—who after more than sixty years in this country still hadn't gotten a firm grasp on the English language—would have called a *chip-a-sket*. So the poor kid's problems continued with his haircut, which was administered by his mother once a week with the aid of a bowl and what seemed to be a pair of dull pruning shears.

"My dad says, 'Why should I pay ten bits to take you down to that crook Maroni when your mother can do a better job right here in our kitchen,'" Teddy would tell us while trying to cover his entire misshapen head with spindly little fingers.

Although head covering in church was mandatory for girls, the nuns forbade any type of headwear for boys inside the building. For a while, the prospect of being able to hide his mother's handiwork had poor Teddy looking into converting to Hassidic Judaism.

His female counterpart, Lisa Thomaselli, had the opposite problem of never remembering to bring her mantilla, a lacy scarf that most of the girls preferred to wearing hats or babushkas to school on church days. That chronic lapse of memory resulted in the nuns, tsking as they went along, placing a tissue on Lisa's head and attaching it with bobby pins. The finished product looked as dorky as Teddy's haircut, leading the rest of the class to speculate on the possibility of a future union between the classmates with the strange heads.

My obvious answer to what Mr. Manfredi perceived as a rhetorical question about "that crook" Maroni would have been, "Because your wife is obviously a victim of Parkinson's disease, macular degeneration, or both." But no ten-year-old but me would think of that and couldn't have pronounced it even if he had.

Teddy was also victimized by his father's frugality in the area of fashion. He generally came to school in clothes that had been handed down from his older brother, Artie, a sixth-grader who, even though the clothes were new when he got them, was no *Gentleman's Quarterly* cover boy himself.

It seemed that Mr. Manfredi's strategy was to buy Artie's clothes a size or two too large, so that he would get more wear out of them as he grew. That not only boded ill for Artie who, when his clothes were new, resembled a two-legged broomstick in a potato sack, but also for his younger brother. After a couple of years, when the buttons started to pop off and the pants split every time Artie bent over, Teddy would get his wardrobe, patched and sewn by his mother. Was there no end to this woman's talents?

While my friend and I, along with the rest of the class, certainly noticed Teddy, he was little more than a curiosity until one day in October when he walked up to us while we were huddled together planning some serious dodgeball strategy on the blacktopped parking lot that served as our playground.

"You guys are always together, huh?" Teddy said in a tone that would have been offensive if we knew enough to be offended.

"Yeah, I guess," Billy replied, then went back to laying out a plan designed to give us the best chance of nailing yucky old Margaret Lerner in the nose when we had the ball. Margaret's lack of a Y chromosome, as well as her status as the nuns' favorite, automatically made her the enemy, thereby condemning her to all manner of vicious retribution from those of us on the outside looking in.

But back to the Teddy Manfredi story.

"I can name all fifty state capitals," he blurted out after a five-second lull.

"Wow," I said without looking up.

He must have taken that as a sign of interest because he immediately launched into the list, alphabetically by state no less. Right around Carson City, Nevada, the noise was starting to get annoying, and I turned around and gave him my best cold stare, a technique that I learned from Matt Dillon on *Gunsmoke*. That guy could stare down a bad guy like nobody else on television, and I spent at least fifteen minutes a day practicing in the mirror in case I ran across any bad guys. Teddy Manfredi was the closest I had come, so I thought I would give it a try.

Evidently, I had mastered the skill better than I thought because the stare put Teddy in a panic, and he immediately began simultaneously trembling, hyperventilating, and crying silently with his mouth wide open. That less-than-appealing sight brought Sister Immaculata over to where we were standing, demanding to know what all the fuss was about.

"Why are you crying, Theodore?" she asked, a tone more of annoyance than concern.

"He ... he ... he," Teddy blubbered, pointing in my direction and crying too hard to finish the sentence.

"I should have known," the nun said in a tone that would have melted a boulder, "I will see you after school, Missssster Scuro."

When a nun called you *mister*, you knew you were in for it. When there were that many S's in it, it was enough to turn your hair gray at ten. And the beauty of the nun criminal justice system was that there were so many possible punishments—kneeling on a hard linoleum floor, writing a one-sentence apology on the chalkboard one hundred or more times, clapping erasers after school—that during the waiting period between conviction and sentencing, you could go crazy trying to figure out which one it would be. It didn't take me long to find out this time. The good sister loaded down the rest of the class with instructions to pull out their rosary beads and pray for the poor children in Africa who have not had the opportunity and the privilege of being introduced to God the Father and His Son, Jesus Christ, who died for our sins. Evidently the denial of proper food and healthcare to those same children wasn't worth the prayers. She was then ready to deal with me. She took me out in the hall and, after explaining under which sins group my behavior had fallen, all venial and no mortal, thank God, lowered the boom. She told me exactly what my punishment would be. (More on mortal vs. venial sin later too.)

"You will apologize personally to Theodore," she began, "and you will stay after school to erase the chalkboards and clean the erasers all of next week."

As soon as the words were out of her mouth, a red-hot poker of fear pierced my heart. The first half of the punishment would be a breeze. I'd go up to Teddy, make gestures and facial expressions that looked like I was expressing sincere contrition for whatever grievous offense I had committed against him, his family, and any future descendants he might sire, while telling him that if he ever got me into trouble again, I would pull his pants down in front of the waiting line for the girls bathroom and pull his oversized, threadbare shirt over his head so he would not have proper use of his hands to pull them back up. After I did that, Teddy once again started to sob uncontrollably. When Sister Immaculata saw this, she walked over, opened her mouth to say something to me, then just rolled her eyes and walked away.

It wasn't the chalkboard-and-eraser punishment that I feared. Not that it was a hard job—Gino had to do it so often, my parents had to take out insurance on him for white lung—it was the fact that it was after school. This meant that I would miss the school bus home, and my parents would have to

know about the crime and the punishment because they would have to pick me up from school.
Specifically, since my mother didn't drive (I always assumed she wanted to be like the nuns),
my dad would have to take off work early to haul
me home.

That drive, I knew, would be accompanied by
daily lectures on how hard he worked to give me a
proper Catholic education, only to have me disgrace
him by "acting up" and causing the good Sisters
no small amount of grief. You see, my father, I was
reminded each day, didn't have it as easy as I did.
His father made a living by picking rags out of
garbage bins and sewing them together by hand to
make elegant coats, which he sold to rich people for
fifty cents a pop. Apple sellers were a dime a dozen
in the twenties; my grandfather was a real crafts-
man. It didn't take many of these sad stories for me
to realize that the only generation in our nation's
history that had it tougher than the one that grew up
during the Great Depression was the next generation, that had to hear about how agonizing it was.

Billy was waiting for me when I went out to catch the bus. Sister had granted me a one-day parole to tell my parents that I needed to be picked up after school for a week.

"What did you do to Manfredi?" he asked with a combination of incredulity and admiration in his voice.

"I just gave him my Matt Dillon stare," I said while extending my arms, palms upraised in a gesture of my own disbelief.

"Then you musta nailed that one," he said. "I'm pretty sure he peed his pants."

"No loss there," I mused absently.

Chapter 4

My Family

WHEN I got home from school that afternoon, looking sullen and scared despite my best efforts to hide both emotions, my mother, in her own uncanny way, didn't notice. She looked up from one of her "stories" on television, with a look that reminded me how many times she had told me that she loved these fifteen-minute soap operas—*Search for Tomorrow* and *The Guiding Light* were her favorites—more than she loved me, my father, my brother, and the dog combined.

She then told me that I could have a glass of milk, but if I spoiled my appetite for dinner, I would be in big trouble. Nothing I ever did as a child—or an adult, for that matter—resulted in my getting into "small" trouble, and nothing ever spoiled my appetite for any snack or meal. Having that instinctive ten-year-old's feeling that the milk would probably curdle in my stomach and kill me, I went straight up to the room I shared with Gino.

What I really wanted, although Mom had never thought to ask, was a hunk of the chocolate cake that we had for dessert the night before. But I knew that would never fly, and even if it did, my mother would have insisted on slicing it in her own patented way, which was to take an eight-inch round cake and get enough slices to feed a mission full of homeless people for a week. You could read a newspaper through those slices.

After school was my favorite time to hide in our bedroom because Gino always came home from school much later than I did due to his participation in after-school activities like cross-country, basketball, baseball, and detention.

When Gino wasn't in it, the room was a safe haven where I could be the cool ten-year-old I knew I was with little interference from the people who thought I wasn't. No less than a forty-by-twenty jammed dresser, or "chester drawers," as my parents called them, would block Gino's efforts to enter the room. And then there was the all-important RCA hi-fi record player that my brother had bought with money earned from doing odd jobs for creepy old Mrs. Gigliotti.

But maybe the neatest feature of the room was the spacious walk-in closet, suitable for hiding out with my thoughts and gaining a little respite from the frenetic pace of life at the Scuro house. The long, narrow space was sparsely lined on one side with my clothes and Gino's and jammed on the other side with my mother's old "skinny" clothes that she was sure she would again fit into someday. The floor on both sides was covered with cardboard boxes sloppily labeled "Christmas decs," or "Tax rets," followed by the year of filing. The boxes made for an even greater cushion when I was small but got to be a little harder to work around when I started my freakish growth spurt. But even when Gino would shove me into this mothball-reeking inner sanctum and push the dresser up against the door so I couldn't escape, I enjoyed the time spent in my private little clubhouse.

The period between my arrival home from school and the frightening, always unwelcome arrival of my much older sibling was my solace time. It was my chance to play Gino's records without hearing from the nuns or my parents that it was a sin to listen to rock 'n' roll at my tender age or an admonition from my brother that he would rip my face off if I ever touched any of his stuff again. Fortunately for me, Gino wasn't bright enough to notice if his possessions had been disturbed unless he was right there to see it happen. Even then I could sometimes pull it off. Sin or not, I was rocking out to Elvis, Jerry Lee, and Little Richard, while most of my classmates were humming Disney tunes.

My favorite part of this grand solitude was lip-syncing to the records and emulating the moves I had seen on *The Ed Sullivan Show* when I was supposed to be doing my homework. By now, I also knew I had to be careful when to go into my act. Once, when I thought they were engrossed in *Dragnet*, my mother burst into tears while my father told me that he was calling the "nut house" to come and take me away because only a lunatic would act like that all by himself. I never quite understood the underlying message that if there were other people in attendance while I was gyrating around the room with a hairbrush microphone,

I would be sane. That was the interaction between my parents and me. It reminds me of a quote from someone. (I don't know who. It was probably Mark Twain, Winston Churchill, or Yogi Berra. They seem to be credited with all the quotes since the beginning of time.) But again, I digress. As I recall, the quote was, "When I was young, I thought that my father was an idiot, but as I grew older, I was amazed at how smart the old man had become." My dad has been dead for six years, and that still hasn't happened. Sorry, Pop!

But God bless his pointy little head, he tried. Because, as I may have mentioned, my mother didn't drive, it fell to Dad to give me my driving lessons.

"It's a waste of time to take Driver's Ed in school," he reasoned. "That time can be spent doing homework, doing your chores, running to the icebox to get me beers, or watching the Steelers' next loss so you can update me on the other team's scoring drive while I'm in the can."

And so it was that my driver's lessons began under the supervision of a man who washed down antacids with Stoney's beer while in the car teaching me to drive. (And here's a bit of trivia for you. Stoney Jones, founder and owner of Stoney's beer, was the father of movie star and future mother of *The Partridge Family*, Shirley Jones. Riveting stuff, huh?)

So, I drove, and I parallel parked with the help of a broken rearview mirror. I drove the serpentine through an obstacle course of the neighbor's garbage cans like I, not my father, was the drunken party in the car. Meanwhile, under the influence of the Stoney's, Dad snoozed and would occasionally open one eye and mutter, "Good job, son, very good job."

I failed my first driving test administered by a sober Pennsylvania state trooper with flying colors. My second go-round, with an officer I suspected wasn't so sober, went better. He sloppily signed my learner's permit, told me that I would get my license in four to six weeks, and muttered that it was lunchtime. Liquid?

When I got back to the station, beaming and showing my father my signed certificate, he said, "Yeah, well you might have fooled that cop, but you don't fool me. You're grounded until I give you more lessons."

A regular Knute Rockne, my pop was.

Self-esteem hadn't been invented yet when I was a kid. As with many new inventions, I wonder if we haven't taken things a bit too far these days. But I still think fondly of the mother of a high school friend who took an interest in me and gave me a couple of compliments I replay in my head to this day. Sadly, she is gone now. Her interest made a difference to me, as stupid as that sounds. I didn't get a lot of that. I later tried to pass that gift on to my kids' friends, as did their mother, a creature so perfect their friends called our house the "Donna Reed house."

Then there was my extended family. Thirteen cousins on my father's side and six on my mother's —what a piker, huh?

These are the families that would visit each other's homes at least once a week for a huge meal. These visits were sometimes for birthdays or holidays, meals that were so special that the don't-even-ask-for-a-glass-of-water restriction was lifted.

The once-a-week cousins were a family of girls except for the baby, who would stay inside to be coddled and spoiled alternately by one or two of his sisters at a time. The rest of us would play tag, hide-and-seek, king of the hill, or touch football. Since the touch football games were me against the girls, they were my favorites.

These visits were often punctuated with little spats that sometimes turned into yelling and crying sessions. Since I was told by my macho father that men don't cry, these were also my favorite times.

These tiffs were often over games. "You're a cheater" was the most commonly heard phrase, followed by "no fair" and "I want a Mulligan." I was duly impressed by the girls' knowledge of the golf reference.

I enjoyed these visits with playmates who could do more than grunt monosyllabically and crush me, like my ape of a big brother. Gino was built like a fire hydrant and could never go out wearing red or yellow, lest every male dog in the neighborhood would see him as an opportunity to relieve himself. (That actually happened once—I laughed until I cried, then cried some more when Gino picked me up by my shirt collar, lifted me over his head, and dropped me on mine.) Fun and games aside, like us all, my mother's-side cousins were also dosed early with the guilt and fear that served to keep kids tractable. Case in point: my cousin James, who had landed in the "slow" class for the dreaded "not living up to his potential," was miraculously cured with a single gesture after a parent-nun conference one day.

He sat in the back seat of the car (relax, that was okay back in the day), waiting for his mother to finish speaking with the nun, imagining the worst. As she emerged from the building to walk back to the car, he inspected her face closely for any sign of how much trouble he was in. She shook her head once, her mouth a grim line. Not long thereafter, James was in the advanced class, his "potential" suddenly freed from its bonds. After they grew up, my mother's-side cousins divided equally into "Praise-Jee-zus" Evangelicals, breaking their Catholic parents' hearts, and what comic Jim Gaffigan calls "Shiite Catholics."

My father's-side cousins morphed into radical liberals, especially in the cause of feminism. Now, I bow to no one in supporting the feminist cause, but these nuts are what that moron Rush Limbaugh used to call "feminazis." Ironically, they are as bad as the nuns when it came to spurning the male of the species. Every time anyone would make a disparaging remark about a woman, no matter how true, these folks would say with an ear-piercing shriek, "You wouldn't say that about a man!"

"Would so."

One of them has decided that she is an insult comic. She is, however, nowhere close. I keep trying to tell her that (A) the insult should be subtle. It should take the insultees at least ten seconds to realize they have been insulted. And (B), most importantly, one does not cackle like a hen the moment the insult is delivered. Groucho Marx never said, "I see you standing in front of a hot stove, but I can't see the stove. Ha ha ha ha ha." It's just not done. I have begged her to move on to something more constructive, like counting the number of species that have become extinct since the beginning of time.

Chapter 5

As Promised, More About Confession

So, YOU want to know more about confession? Well, I never break a promise, so you're gonna hear it anyway.

Confession is the second sacrament of the Catholic Church, immediately following baptism, which at one time had to be administered to newborn babies soon after birth. I find no fault with this, since the little poop machines have no idea what's going on except they're being held by strangers selected by their parents to be god-mother and godfather. These are individuals the little tyke will probably never see again after they have sucked up all the food and booze at the party thrown by the parents to commemorate this happy occasion.

The initial reason this was necessary was so the child could be taken immediately to heaven and not spend all eternity in limbo, which I previously mentioned, is now permanently closed. That declaration was made—by, can you believe it?—Pope Benedict XVI, the ultraconservative who succeeded Pope John Paul II, the first non-Italian pope in 455 years after the murder of Pope John Paul I after only thirty-three days as pontiff.

And don't tell me he wasn't murdered. There is a tell-all book written by a former mafioso named Anthony Raimondi who says he aided in the assassination on behalf of his cousin Paul Marcinkus, an American who was president of the Vatican Bank. The motive, he says, was that the pope threatened to expose the stock fraud committed by Marcinkus and about half the College of Cardinals. His Holiness threatened to expose and excommunicate the offenders and defrock the clergy involved. According to Raimondi, he studied the habits of John Paul I and reported them to his cousin. Marcinkus then laced the pope's regular evening tea with cyanide.

The Vatican physician declared that the pope died of a heart attack (yeah, sure), and according to the website, "Pope John Paul II kept his mouth shut, so he lived."

Once again, I have drifted off the main point, but it's pretty interesting, don't you think?

What really galled those of us of the Italian persuasion about the non-Italian pope was that he was *Polish*. Seriously? It just seemed wrong somehow. Maybe Greek to stay in the Mediterranean region or Swiss so he spoke the same language, but Polish, nah!

Now back to confession.

The reason I referred to the confessional as "the box of horrors" is because it was a four-by-four room with a door and no ventilation, which increased the already inevitable flop sweats that would occur when the Reverend Father would finish with the poor slob on the other side. The priest would recline in a comfortable chair in his larger box between that of the penitents—I peeked inside once—while we who have sinned had to kneel on rock-hard kneelers. The priest always claimed that we were anonymous, but I knew he could tell from my freakishly husky voice that it was me. Megan O'Toole, who had an unusually low voice for a girl, always got honked off when Father would call her "my son." Now, once he doled out the other person's penance—Our Fathers, Hail Marys, a rosary or two if the offense was exceptionally heinous, it was my turn.

"Bless me, Father, for I have sinned. It has been one week since my last confession." It better not have been longer than that. "I have lied eight times."

I have to stop and explain this. Somehow the church must have expected its prepubescent sinners to keep a record of the number of times you have committed a particular sin, making it necessary for you to keep some kind of a journal to keep up. This meant that you had to either memorize it or read it in the dark of the box of horrors. Once I tried to smuggle in a tiny flashlight I had gotten in a box of cereal, but Father McClatchy noticed it and tacked on more prayers to my sentence ... er, penance. So, I continued, "I sassed my mother nine-and-a-half times, not ten because she laughed at one of them, I never sassed my father because the punishment for that would be of the corporal variety. I hated my stinking brother more times than Einstein could count, and I didn't rob any liquor stores"—more penance for being a wiseacre.

Now back to penance. The standard penance usually included a number of Our Fathers, Hail Marys, and Glory Bes. Presumably, in the more heinous cases, I'm guessing murder, grand theft auto, stock fraud (I bet Mr. Marcinkus got nailed hard on that one) that weren't generally committed by seven-year-olds, if the good Father was old school, you might get a penance of tar and feathering or a hair shirt. Although Father McClatchy was new-school and our sins relatively minor, you could spend the rest of a perfectly good Saturday afternoon kneeling in a pew saying your designated prayers. I missed a lot of TV shows that way. Although I haven't been to confession in the past thirty-plus years, I still get pangs of anxiety when I think about it.

Chapter 6

A Tale of Romance?

So far, this tale of mine has been all sweetness and light. Now it could get a little pathetic.

When I somehow made it to sixth grade on schedule, I fell head over heels for the first time. During that summer, I discovered that boys and girls were different. (Kids learn that now at about five years old because of "progressive" parents who send them to Montessori schools where, presumably, they stare at each other naked, then write essays about what they learned.) We weren't nearly as sophisticated or repulsive. I made the mistake that summer of asking Gino to give me some clue about this weighty matter, and he gleefully responded by showing me his hidden collection of *Hustler* magazines. Then I realized that Gino and Larry Flynt were every bit as repulsive as the Montessori schools. But I did get a glimpse of what the girls were hiding under their clothes, and it answered a question or two.

So, I entered the sixth grade as an enlightened pervert.

Then it happened. I saw this beautiful vision as soon as I walked into the room on the first day of classes. Her name was Gemma Napolitano, as lovely as the Venus de Milo, with an Italian name. That, my friends, is perfection.

Gemma had actually joined us in the fourth grade, but I took no notice because I was still young and naïve. Well, I take that back. I felt a pang every time Sister Monica confiscated for herself the salami sandwich she could smell in Gemma's lunch bag. Along with having the "the calling," a status elicited from kids eager to please by nuns and priests with the hopeful relentlessness of a multilevel marketing scheme, nuns seem to have been required to pass a rigorous olfactory-sense test. More about that later. "This isn't good for you," Sister would say, whisking away from Gemma the redolent, wax-papered, slightly grease-stained package (Genoa salami, you know) and replacing it with a PB and J, hastily made in the church basement kitchen and dished up on a paper napkin. Sister appeared to have been seeking indulgences, a sort of holy brownie points, by consuming the unwholesome salami herself, as was evident to anyone coming within a yard of her. Any attempt to address this directly would have been considered an almost sacrilegious affront. Gemma never said a word, but a scrap of peanut-butter-stained napkin returned in the lunch bag may have signaled the truth. Gemma's mother had tried giving Sister Monica a salami for Christmas, but the thievery hadn't stopped. The good Sister also nobly consumed fruit kids unknowingly brought in with invisible—but no doubt dangerous—"bad spots."

But now the pang in my gut was of another type entirely. There Gemma stood, tall and willowy at a perfect five-foot-one with a not-so-Italian straw-berry-blonde ponytail and light skin with freckles, wearing the plaid skirt and white blouse the girls were required to wear along with lacy white ankle socks at Holy Cross, the loveliest sight I had ever seen. (Big sigh!)

I was nervous about approaching this goddess in a school uniform, but I mustered up all my courage, assumed a confident pose, approached her with my coolest saunter, and promptly proceeded to trip over my desk/chair and fall on my face at her feet. I tried to hide my embarrassment, got up, and was about to assure her that she didn't have to worry, I was all right. Then it occurred to me that that wasn't necessary because she had never asked the question. She just looked down on me, rolled her eyes, and sat down. Intrepid as I was, I moved my desk/chair closer to hers, which prompted her to move the other way. I tried one more time and got the same reaction and then decided I'd better quit because her next move would have been outside on the playground.

The rest of that day was a blur. Sister Mary Immaculata must have employed some of her special nun ESP, because she started firing questions at me that she knew I could never answer, like "What's your name, Enzo?" and "Who's buried in Grant's tomb?" Those both threw me for a loop. "Am I boring you, Enzo? Or is your head in the clouds?" she inquired. I know she actually wanted to say, "up your butt," but that would have gotten her a wazoo of penance.

After a few "no stirs," I decided to get a little creative.

"To tell you the truth, Sister," I lied through my teeth, "my mother had to take my dog, Capone, to the vet this morning, and I'm afraid they're going to have to put him down." I had decided quickly not to use the old "my grandmother died" routine because I couldn't remember how many times I had used it before. Unless your parents were each married multiple times—a no-no in the Catholic Church—more than two was excessive.

After a moment's hesitation, she must have decided to reluctantly believe me. "Mmm," she mused, "interesting name for a dog, but I guess it makes sense." Then she continued. "Pets are our trusted friends who love us unconditionally. I remember when my beloved kitty cat, Holy Ghost, later changed to Holy Spirit, died at the tender age of twenty-two. I thought I would die too, but of course, I didn't."

"Evidently, Stir," I said.

"Of course, I was much younger then," she said with a wry smile. "I was young once, you know, Enzo."

In my mind, I was saying "hard to believe," and "I hate cats." Out loud I said, "Of course, Stir."

"But you children must be brave young men and women and realize that animals do not live as long as humans. I am sure that Capone would want you to keep up with your studies so that you will be the best *you* possible."

What the ...? "Yes, Stir."

Chapter 7

Billy Is Gone

OUR MADCAP adventures at Holy Cross continued in well-worn grooves. My freakish size, deep voice, and the mouth I couldn't seem to control made me a lightning rod for nunly wrath, frequently manifested upon my knuckles, which are not quite right even today. (Yes, possibly cracking my knuckles, an unfortunate habit I adopted in later years, had something to do with that, but I maintain that it was a way of reasserting hegemony over my metacarpals and phalanges. That is my story, and I am sticking to it.) On the other hand— literally—Billy's knuckles were pristine, although

his timidity and soft-spoken replies would sometimes irritate Sister Agnes, who may have had a
hearing issue. She had no "inside voice," as we say
these days. At times Billy would come out of his
shell a bit, but at other times he would retreat beyond reaching. Even my antics couldn't bring him
out. Eventually, even I finally got it through my
thick head that too many questions would make
my friend shut down.

Each summer, my once-a-week cousins and I
spent time—separately, as there were a lot of us—
at our other cousins' house, slightly north and out
of our more citified environment. I looked forward
to these visits; I was intrigued by my older cousins,
and Aunt Maria could cook like an angel.

I had been startled to see that my cousin Donna,
a rebel in her own time, had vaguely resembled a
molting sheep. Upon arriving at high school as a
freshman, she had ever-so-slightly backcombed and
added a touch of AquaNet to her hair to yield the
distinctive "bump" you see in class photo arrays
of the time. Rules were laid down on day one. No
hairspray or teasing, no makeup, no nail polish.
Sister Cecilia had walked the aisles, right hand
touching the heads of the girls on the right, left

hand inspecting the girls on the left, and Donna's hair having given the telltale sign of stiffness, she had been sent off to the bathroom with, she said, a bar of "disgusting lard." I conjured up visions of gas-station soap, covered in filthy black cracks.

She tried just rinsing out the AquaNet, but that didn't fly. Sister sniffed her head—olfactory senses in Franciscan nuns were evidently on a par with our Ursuline salami-sniffing nuns—and sent her back to apply the foul-smelling bar. Returning to the classroom, Sister had brutally brushed out the resulting tangled mess in a single stroke, using a brush that bristled with what seemed like a generation of unfortunate girls' hair in all colors. Donna's hair came out in clumps, glistening as it floated down in the light streaming through the windows. She sat in class humiliated, trying to cover her bald spots, as Sister Cecilia lectured on kindness to others with no trace of irony. Donna had never dared sneak makeup, as the Sisters had a beauty-school sized inventory in cotton balls, baby oil, and nail polish remover and would "help" the offending girl roughly scrub the last trace from their faces or hands. Thereafter, Donna was a target of grim suspicion by the Sisters, so much so that her allergy inhaler, resembling a Chapstick, had her hauled before the school authorities like a criminal.

Donna gave me my first puff of a cigarette on that visit. I didn't like it much at the time, truthfully, but basked in the grown-up feeling. This vice too Donna had to keep well away from school. It seems that one Sister Alberta was built along the lines of a defensive tackle for the Green Bay Packers. (The girls called her "Big Berta" in whispers.) Sister Alberta had sniff-test duty at the end of the recess period to root out the sinful smokers. A hapless kid named Derek had tempted fate and failed the sniff test. Sister Alberta had rolled up her sleeve, with various nunly things dangling from the rolled-up cuff, said to Derek, "This is your last warning," and sucker-punched him, his head banging hard against the church windows as he slid down the wall to the floor like a barroom brawl scene in a Western. No medical professionals were called, as would happen today—there was no head injury reporting. Derek just sat in the scarily silent class for the rest of the day.

Patchy hair and PTSD or no, I liked Donna a lot. Still do. After those stories, I understood why she secretly carted Pickles the Bear with her every time she took a trip. Sometimes humans are just too awful to be borne.

The other attraction of these summer visits was a custard stand, the real thing, which is still open today. I make the pilgrimage every time I can find anyone crazy enough to drive with me a skosh more than forty miles each way for custard.

When I got back from my summer adventure, on an overcast sweltering Saturday, family greetings were brief. We were not a hug-and-kiss I-love-you family, something I had seen and envied at friends' houses, places I preferred infinitely to my own, where tension hung in the air. I swore my own kids would be raised differently, and I would later keep that promise.

After the volume and degree of dirtiness of my incoming laundry had been exclaimed over with displeasure by my mother, and my father had inquired about his siblings, sighing worriedly after each piece of the status report was delivered, I was ready to escape the soul-sucking atmosphere in the Scuro house. I knew at least Billy would be glad to see me. He always dreaded the summer, although he never said so right out. He didn't need to. I instinctively understood no school meant he would be unrelievedly under the "care" of his stepmother, without even the relative kindness of the nuns. I had two formerly crisp dollar bills carefully folded in my pocket, one from each of my uncles, silent expressions of solidarity and gratitude for a male branch on our overwhelmingly female family tree. I had change for streetcar fare. I would bring my much-prized baseball glove. Billy and I could throw a ball around and get ice cream, maybe a burger.

I had just finished lunch—tuna salad sandwiches, Wise potato chips, and milk—but was already starting to get hungry again. Keeping me in food and the clothes I outgrew in no time was a sore trial for my parents. The one bright spot for my overworked mother was that I was fast becoming the designated sandwich-maker in the house. My father, brother, and even my grandfather, who pronounced it "sangwich," would often send me to the kitchen during games and nighttime TV viewing. I was always up for a sandwich and took care in creating whatever each person wanted, with proper proportions of meat, condiments, bread, lettuce, and thinly sliced tomato. To this day, feeding people is one of my greatest pleasures.

"I'm going to see what Billy is doing," I said, heading to the hallway for the phone.

We had exchanged phone numbers long ago, at my initiation, but Billy had never called me. I had called him twice during the school year, once on a Saturday to see if he wanted to come over and watch Pitt play WVU with my dad, my uncle, my brother, and me—the mood in our house lifted to something resembling festive on game days—and once when he had been unexpectedly absent from school. The first time, the line was busy, and I never got through, in spite of my top-notch dialing skills honed by calling radio stations for prizes. The second call had been answered by a female, presumably his stepmother, who listened to my polite introduction without comment, informed me that Billy was doing his homework, and disconnected.

"Son," my father said, stopping until I swiveled back around to look at him, "Billy's not home. He went to live with family out of state."

My brain tried to process the words, whirling and roaring as it searched for any translation other than the obvious meaning of the sounds my ears had just heard. My stomach felt hollow.

"Why?" I said, hearing my voice an octave higher than my prematurely husky voice of late. So much

for my grownup adventures and sophisticated cigarette puffs. I was too flabbergasted to say anything
else, and besides, it would have delayed the answer I
needed *now*.

"Something about his stepmother; she's not
doin' too good."

So, she had finally found a way to get rid of him,
after torturing him all this time. My fury erupted. "She sent him *away*? She's a witch! I hope she
dies!"

My father slapped me sharply, the pain searing
my cheek and blotting out everything else for a
minute. "I don't ever want to hear you talk like that
again." He said it quietly, but his tone was harsh and
urgent. The shock and the injustice of both blows,
the news and the slap, overwhelmed me, and now I
was bawling outright. "Do you want to go to hell? Is
that what you want?" he asked, holding my shoulders so I was forced to look at him.

I twisted away and yelled, "I am in hell! Right
now! You don't know what she did to him! *Where
is he?*" I roared. I would find my friend. Maybe I
would run away and go join him. I had my Commu-
nion money under a loose floorboard I found one
day while locked in my closet, after reading a book

called *The Borrowers*. I didn't find any little people living there, but I did find a perfect spot to hide things from my oaf of a brother, who lacked my intimate knowledge of our closet.

"With an aunt, I think, somewhere in Wisconsin. He's not coming back, Enzo. Let it go."

Wisconsin. I could see myself rooting for the Packers with my friend. Packers fans were as nuts as Steelers fans. "Did he leave a number? Did he say he would call back?" I could go downtown to the Greyhound station and take a bus—I looked older than my age, and grownups tended to leave me alone. I could easily concoct a story if I needed to.

"He didn't call. I heard at the mine."

Billy's father worked in the mine also. Maybe Billy asked his dad to find my dad and tell him.

"Did his dad tell you?"

"No, I heard from some of the guys. I said, leave it *alone*, Enzo."

My father's emphasis on the word "alone" showed he was getting irritated. I dared not risk another slap. "We're going out for dinner tonight, to give your mother a break with all that laundry you brought home. Be cleaned up and ready to go by quarter of six."

And that was the last I would hear of Billy. I went by his house a few times. Although his neighborhood was tonier than mine, his home was a depressing-looking row house with a door badly in need of painting and windows that looked like they hadn't been cleaned since the Truman administration. I planned to give Teddy's name to avoid my father's wrath if I was able to speak to anyone and get Billy's whereabouts, but the doorbell echoed in silence each time. On my last visit, a For Rent sign had been placed in the window, and my last hope of finding my friend vanished.

Chapter 8

Finally, the Reunion

As I twiddled my thumbs in the car and was about to give up, the huge, heavy doors to the ancient stone edifice opened, and out walked Billy, flanked by two burly men in uniform and wearing an ill-fitting blue suit that was standard issue for felons who had served their time.

He was even skinnier and paler than I remembered him when we were kids, but even at this distance, I could see those bright-blue eyes still held the same fascination.

And then it all came flooding back to me, memory that I had pushed far to the back of my head so the guilt didn't drive me nuts.

It was a conversation with my father shortly before he died. He was already collecting disability because of years working down in that damnable pit so that people who lived comfortably above could heat their houses and a few, even in the mid-sixties, could cook their food.

It brought back to my mind the Jimmy Dean song, "Big Bad John," which he recorded before he started selling sausages.

The big, strong man who raised me was now a shadow of himself. Just two years before, he had been heavy enough that he couldn't go along when he took Angelica, Gino's youngest, horseback riding. Angelica had, thankfully, inherited her mother's intelligence, and the normal human compassion that had skipped her father had been passed down to her in spades. The kid wouldn't play board games for fear she would win (which she would have) and hurt someone's feelings. When the stable owner eyed my father up and down and broke the news that he couldn't ride one of his horses, sweet Angelica had flung her arms around him, devastated by the injustice, and said with her big eyes welling up, "Oh, Pop-Pop!"

In that moment I swore I would one day be a Pop-Pop. But those days were long gone. He was now so pale, he was almost translucent, so thin you could count his ribs through his T-shirt. My father now could no longer even do justice to his favorite meal, my mother's eye of round roast with spaghetti. (Not penne, not rigatoni—spaghetti.) I still make that meal when he is on my mind.

He looked up at me, a more serious look than I had ever seen, and said, "Son, I have something to talk to you about, and it's very, very serious."

"What is it, Pop? You're weirding me out."

"It's about Billy," he said, "Billy Tildon."

"What about Billy?"

"You know his old man died about a month ago, right?"

"Sure, Pop," I said, a little amazed. "We all went to the funeral, remember?"

"Of course, I remember. I'm dying, I don't have Altsbergers. Billy didn't go to live with relatives."

"What do you mean?" I said, puzzled, casting my mind back. My father had warned me not to ask about Billy at the funeral, saying he had "run off" from his aunt's and the rest of the family didn't know where he was. For a change, I had listened;

but I hoped my friend would find a way to contact me, and for a few weeks, I leapt for the phone when it rang, to no avail. But if he hadn't gone to live with relatives...where was he? Could he have died, and my father didn't tell me? Maybe he got hurt, like the oldest D'Angelo boy, who was paralyzed when he drove his motorcycle into a parked car at a high rate of speed and now had to live in some kind of facility. Every Christmas the family would pile into the car to make the drive to see Domenic. I never had any desire to ride a motorcycle after that.

"He's okay, isn't he?"

"He's in prison, Enzo. He has been all this time. He killed his stepmother."

"He what?" I had heard the words, but it was not computing. Billy was so softhearted he once begged me to let fireflies out of a jar so they wouldn't be scared.

"When you were at Aunt Maria's that summer. There were a bunch of stories, but supposedly she got hit in the head with a heavy ashtray. I dunno."

"Oh my God," I said, replaying that summer in my head. It finally made sense. "Pop, she was evil. She beat him with a switch if she thought he looked sad, and she laughed at him for crying and missing his mom. She would say, *Aw, does the poor widdle baby miss his mommy?* She told his father he was weak and needed to be toughened up or she'd put a dress on him. She would burn him with cigarettes and laugh and say, *Be a man, you little sissy.* His dad just let her!" My anger was growing as I remembered. I left out some of the more horrific details I began to recall—my ill father didn't need to know just how twisted a human can be. "Oh my God. Poor Billy. I should have done something."

"Son," my father said, with more energy in his voice than I had heard in a very long time, "you couldn't have done anything. In those days, they thought children needed a woman, and his dad did the best he could. He didn't know what else to do."

"He would have been better off being raised by wolves," I said. "So where is he?"

"He's in the penitentiary."

"Still? I'm pretty sure some of the Nazi war criminals got less time than that. They should have pinned a medal on him."

"Watch your mouth," my father said sharply. "I'm sorry for your friend, Enzo, but a lot of kids have it tough, and they don't kill anyone. Didn't you learn anything at that expensive school I sent you to?" The old man had a point. I was silent. I couldn't square it with the gentle soul I knew. Something must have happened.

"He'll be getting out soon. I dunno why he's still there." My father shrugged. He was not one to question authority, unless you counted referees and umpires. Priests, doctors, nuns—whatever they said was accepted as fact. "I didn't want you involved in all of that or anyone thinking bad about you."

"I get it," I said. And I did. My father had protected me. Billy had not been so lucky.

"Enzo?" Billy was at the car window, looking tentatively at the grey, balding, bearded, bulky person in the driver's seat. I did not look like the skinny, dark-haired kid he would remember. I debated getting out to hug him, but getting out of the car was a process lately, and I wanted to get him out of there as quickly as possible before the goons who were eyeing us threateningly changed their minds. They likely wanted to get back for the broadcast of the World Series game.

"I know, I'm old. Get in, buddy!" I said, and my friend opened the door, tossed his bag in the back, and slid into the seat next to me. I pointed to the seatbelt, realizing it had been a long time since he was in a car, and he buckled up.

I started driving, feeling safer with each street between us and the dungeon.

I had many questions. What had happened that day with his stepmother? What was prison like? Had he been abused there too? And other questions neither of us could answer, like how would it be possible for Billy to build a life—get a job, find a permanent place to live, make friends? What kind of future could he hope for?

For once, I was able to hold my questions. I said, "Wanna listen to the baseball game?" A huge smile split Billy's face. No response was necessary. I fiddled with the dial and mercifully pulled in the station.

There would be plenty of time to fill in the blanks.

But first, there were sandwiches.

Salami, freshly sliced from the Italian store, not the supermarket, on Mancini's buns. Plenty of mayo. Thinly sliced tomato. Two sandwiches each, with a "family size" bag of chips to share, and orange-and-brown cartons of iced tea.

"Reach behind my seat, buddy—there's some sandwiches in a bag. Grab yourself one and pass one over here if you would."

Billy ripped open the chips and balanced them between us on the console, passed me a sandwich, and started in on his own.

It had been many years since the Pittsburgh Pirates had been called upon to suit up in October, so there was no pain—well, almost none—at listening to the party to which we were not invited. But glancing at Billy's face, surveying the world around him, which had looked so depressing to me, and enjoying America's pastime, it felt like a win to me. It was suddenly a beautiful fall day.

I mentally added "car cleaning, including console" to the list of things I hoped I would one day feel like doing.

Epilogue

LATER WE would learn how right my father was. I was glad he was gone before the reports of abuses in schools and churches began to surface. I personally never experienced any kind of abuse by a priest, unless you count the confessional horrors, which I don't —nor, to the best of my knowledge, did anyone with whom I went to school. But one priest on the attorney general's list had been at a church I attended for a time. So, I take it back—maybe Mark Twain/Winston/Yogi/whoever said that thing about later realizing their father was smart had a point. A lot of kids have it tough and keep it to themselves. As much as we hear about, there are many more kids toughing it out at school or home that we never hear about at all.

It's not hard to figure out why. To voice the injustice means spoiling the happy, picturesque narrative of loved ones and others around them, as well as themselves—the childhood everyone wants to have had, and that others around them seemed to enjoy.

To speak up turns others against them; those they love are unmoved, even disdainful, of the things they have shared, and fight for the memories they want. It is either untrue—they are lying or exaggerating—or they brought it on themselves. They are set apart—they are not like the rest of the family—everyone else is blessedly (or determinedly) happy! The calculation becomes, suffering for their whole lives and renouncing the feeling of belonging in their own worlds, the only one they know, versus secretly suffering for a portion of it. It is no wonder abusers flourish. Kudos to the kids whose hearts refuse to normalize coldness, cunning or cruelty, acknowledged or not, and who continue to give love to others. Their fortunate children will inherit the antibodies rather than the disease.

But back to filling you in on what happened. Billy is adjusting to his new life—there is a lot to tell there.

It turned out that his stepmother's death had been an accident, although he had uncharacteristically been fighting back. She told him he was "ungrateful" for "moaning" about his mother ("*You* killed her," she had said. "If she hadn't had you, she'd be alive now. She probably hated you too.") She had ordered him to bring her ashtray and cigarettes. He put them on the table, and she grabbed his arm. "You stay right here, you little sissy," she hissed. He ducked under the table, dreading the burning. She wouldn't let go of his arm, and she went down to the floor, pulling the tablecloth with her. The ashtray hit her head, which then hit the floor. She had "runny blood," a condition requiring her to take vitamin K before dentist appointments. This was long before blood thinners. The smallest nick requiring the spot-sized Band-Aid could cause a crime-scene amount of blood. With blood everywhere and the mess from the table contents, it looked like a true bloody murder had been underway.

Billy, who had never fought back before, was overcome with guilt. He had run to the neighbor for help, saying, "Please get help! I hurt my stepmom." She was taken to the hospital and seemed to be recovering well, telling everyone within earshot—nurses, doctors, cafeteria and housekeeping staff—that her stepson had tried to kill her.

Two days later, right before she was about to be released, she died unexpectedly from a brain bleed. Billy was then charged with murder, his stepmother's statements at the hospital sealing his fate and yielding the harshest possible penalty. Billy put up no resistance, and his stunned father, having lost two wives and, for all intents and purposes, now his son, had an eighth-grade education and no capacity to aid him. Billy was sent to a notorious juvenile facility, now shut down, whose very name evoked fear and kept generations of kids in line. Kids with mental illness or low IQs were mixed in a volatile stew with kids formed by tough neighborhoods and some who were simply vicious. Drugs were beginning to wreak their havoc. Administrators, many well-meant, others more self-serving, battled to maintain order and exert influence, with political pressures coming from the left and right. The end result was a chaotic powder keg that frequently erupted.

At age twenty-one, Billy was transferred to the penitentiary to serve out his remaining sentence.

After leaving the rented house that had been Billy's hell, his father rented a basement apartment in a house owned by an elderly couple in a neighborhood closer to the mine. He worked every hour he could get, and in his off hours drank steadily, generously tipping the bartenders, smiling obligingly at jokes, and confiding in no one. He visited Billy faithfully until his death. Out of his depth, he had little to say besides, "Are they feeding you all right, son?" But he was there.

Billy stayed at my house for five weeks, on a pull-out couch that we didn't bother to pull out, as the sofa was bed-sized for his small frame. I taught him basic kitchen skills.

We started, of course, with "sangwiches."

Here is part of the repertoire Billy learned, and that will see you and those you love through happy lives.

- A regional specialty, "chipped" ham – shaved or scraped ham morsels that are piled high and somehow far transcend your basic slices. (Woe betide the unlucky deli-counter employee who calls out the number of the scooped-out ticket I have pulled from the red Take-a-Number machine and tries to pass off "thinly sliced" ham as "chipped." I normally regard laziness as an art form, but in matters of chipped ham, I draw the line.) Chipped ham with mayo and tomato on Italian bread, preferably hand-sliced, or with mustard and carefully blotted pickle slices.

- Tuna salad, with very well-drained tuna, generous mayo, dill, celery, finely chopped onion. Best on a toasted Italian roll or bun. This sandwich can also be handy for clearing rooms when you wish to dine alone.
- Club sandwiches with three slices of toast, freshly roasted turkey, bacon, American cheese, lettuce, mayo and—in my house— frilly toothpicks and ruffled chips.

Then the hot variety—they take a minute longer, but never too long for people you love.

- Fried bologna (just a couple of minutes in a pan with a bit of oil), iceberg lettuce, mayo, any bread. Yes, more Michelin Man than Michelin star, but much easier on the budget. Try it.
- Egg-and-pepper, a lunch guaranteed to leave grease stains on the paper bag, a foolproof genetic test performed by school children long before family trees or DNA.
- Steak hoagie—sliced steak, lots of sautéed peppers and onions, cheese, toasted roll, Italian dressing on it, maybe some fries

on the side, or inside, if you are from
around here or it sounds good to you.
(And FYI, this is *the* best post-colonoscopy
fast-breaker known to man or woman—
you deserve the twelve-inch, even if you
can't finish it in one sitting. If this is
your situation, order from Angelo's.
There is no time to cook. This is an
emergency.)

- Hot sausage and pepper, sausage boiled
  first to remove the grease, then cooked
  in homemade sauce, served with grated
  Locatelli on top on any kind of Italian
  bun. Go to an Italian store you trust for
  the hot sausage. Find the one you like.

- Toasted cheese, aka toasty cheese or grilled
  cheese. This, served any time of day or
  night, says love more than any Valentine's
  Day gift ever could. And, of course, we
  covered the variations on American
  classics, hamburgers and hot dogs.

(Just to be clear—I am not a nutritional Lucretia
Borgia. I can whip up a creation to anyone's calorie
or health requirements, or to balance an earlier or

planned blowout. Take care of the ones you love. And make them sangwiches.)

Next, I taught Billy meals, the kind of food my mother cooked.

Mostly Italian dishes, but not all, reflecting the melting-pot neighborhood of Italian, German, and Eastern European immigrants who arrived at Ellis Island like my grandfather.

Billy learned homemade sauce and spaghetti and meatballs, rolled and browned exactingly; stuffed cabbage; lasagna; pasta e fagioli (fahzool, we pronounce it); an egg-and-zucchini dish we call something like gagoots; meatloaf made with barbecue sauce instead of ketchup (a recipe from a retired firefighter in my neighborhood); pork roast cooked with sauerkraut and hot dogs; spinach gently sautéed in, you guessed it, olive oil and garlic. (My personal "aromatherapy" is that cheap trick, garlic sautéing in olive oil. Never mind those Spring Rain air freshener cones with the blue stuff that disappears. What is the blue stuff and where does it go? I find this frightening. But the point is, if you want your house to smell good, get into the kitchen and rattle some pots and pans.)

Last, I taught him how to make wedding soup. Done properly, this is a two-day project, to allow the fat to rise to the top of the broth and be discarded. Scuro wedding soup is made in quantities measured by the number of chickens used, as in, "I made two chickens of wedding soup." Ours is made with the addition of the shredded meat from the chicken used to make the broth (this is considered wedding soup the "poor way"), tiny meatballs that take forever to roll, small *acini de pepe* pasta (pastina or "pastine" to us) and escarole (aka "scarole"), rather than spinach. It is served with plenty of grated Locatelli Romano cheese, an extravagance, but well worth the extra couple of hours of work needed to pay for a hunk. While it takes a lot of effort, a bowl is a fully balanced meal, good any time of day or night.

Billy will not starve.

While I'm on the subject of wedding soup, I'm going to digress for a moment—you're used to it by now—to pass the Scuro recipe, a tradition currently in the safekeeping of a beloved daughter-in-law, on to you. Give it a shot if you can. Others may tell you wedding soup is not served at weddings in Italy, but I personally am closely acquainted with a wedding in the United States where wedding soup was indeed served. That union, involving the lovely daughter of a lovely goddaughter, has proved to be extraordinarily happy. Coincidence? Maybe. You be the judge. It is appropriate for all other occasions as well, or it can be an occasion all by itself. It gets better as the flavors blend, so prepare in advance if you can and refrigerate or freeze.

Scuro Wedding Soup

Broth:

- 1 chicken, 4–6 pounds
- 3–6 ribs celery, including leaves, to taste
- 1–2 large yellow onions, to taste
- 2 tsp. salt, more to taste
- ¼ tsp. garlic powder or 1 garlic clove
- 4-7 quarts water, or enough to cover the chicken in the largest pot you have

Meatballs:

- 1–1.3 lbs. lean ground beef, 90/10 or as close as you can get
- ½ cup plain dried breadcrumbs, more if needed
- ½ cup grated Romano cheese
- 1¼ tsp. dried oregano or to taste
- 2 tbsp. dried parsley

- 1 tsp. garlic salt (or combine salt + garlic powder to taste)
- 2 jumbo eggs or as much as needed of 3 large eggs

1 head of escarole

6 oz. dried pastina (*acini di pepe*) pasta or other very small pasta

For Serving:
- 1 container of good-quality chicken broth to thin the soup after refrigeration, if needed
- Lots of grated Romano (recommend Locatelli Pecorino Romano)

Remove any giblets from the chicken and discard or reserve for another use. Place chicken in a big pot. Cover with water, add salt, and bring to a boil. Add cleaned celery ribs, peeled and halved onion, and ¼ tsp. garlic powder or 1 clove garlic, peeled and lightly smashed. Cover and boil for 1½ hours, then reduce to a simmer until cooked, or all day if you have it (if you have a big chicken and/or a big pot with a lot of water). Let the chicken cool in the broth until cool enough to handle, then strain off the broth, discarding onion, celery and garlic clove, or reserving for another use. Shred chicken by hand, being very careful to remove all the tiny bones. Return shredded chicken to the strained broth and refrigerate broth and chicken overnight, time allowing.

(If you have the luxury of time, the next day) make the meatballs: combine beef, breadcrumbs, eggs, oregano, parsley, garlic salt, and Romano cheese. Too mealy? Add more egg. Too mushy? Add more breadcrumbs. Roll into marble-sized balls. Recruit help for this if you can. This is why you have kids or grandkids. Take pictures.

Wash the escarole—tear off leaves, place in a clean sink of water and agitate, then soak for 10–15 minutes. The sand will sink to the bottom. Remove clean leaves to a colander and tear the green parts into about 1½-inch pieces. Reserve the white, crunchy, slightly bitter parts for another use or discard.

Remove and discard any fat from the refrigerated broth and chicken, place in a pot, and bring to a boil. If you bought a hunk of Romano, add the rind to the pot—just rinse it first and scrape off any paper. Taste for strength and seasoning. If the broth is too weak, cook down for a bit; if it is too strong, add a bit of water. Add salt as needed. Then carefully, to avoid splashing, add the meatballs and cook until they come to the top. Add the escarole, cook for about 20 minutes until wilted. While the escarole is cooking down, in a separate pot, boil the pastina in salted water according to package directions and drain.

Add the cooked pastina to the soup and simmer everything together for an hour or more to let the flavors blend. Serve with lots of grated Romano cheese.

Note on storing: If you used the Romano rind, leave the rind in the soup as you store and reheat it. And beware, when you refrigerate the cooked soup overnight, the pastina will suck up much of the broth, so be prepared to add additional broth the next day.

Play Pavarotti music when cooking or serving, if you are so inclined. (As a note, I have been informed that conducting to "Nessun Dorma" while holding the large knife used to halve the onion and smash the garlic is evidently "not cool" if others are in the kitchen with you.) Or just do a private mental tarantella. You are keeping tradition alive.

Back to Billy now. With no ID, Social Security number, or banking history, Billy may as well have dropped from Pluto, and this was not something that could be remedied quickly. He got hired at a popular restaurant/bar with scant interest in paperwork, drawing on his new confidence in the kitchen, although it is the deep fryer that figures most heavily in their offerings. He found a one-bedroom apartment above a picture-frame store, owned by the brother of a friend. It could use "updating," as they say these days, but it is his; and my household had plenty of extra house paraphernalia to get him started. My smart and kind-hearted sons and their families include him in holiday invitations, and he has invited a nice waitress, a single mom with two boys, to a Pirates game on occasion. They haven't talked about his past yet. Although Billy is innocent, he has a record as a violent criminal, the last words I would think of in connection with him. I worry about how it will affect him, in this and all contexts. It sounds like her ex-husband isn't exactly a box of chocolates, so hopefully she will be able to see his true worth. And he can cook! But if it doesn't work out, he has as much right as any of us to get his heart broken, as much as I would hate to see that happen. He still misses his mom and speaks of her often. I wonder how different his life would have been if she had lived.

The next hurdles for Billy are banking and driving. I tried to open a joint bank account with him at a small local savings bank, but the manager was un-moved by the Dickensian portrait I painted and went from initially friendly to stony before our eyes. I could tell she was eyeing the security button under her desk. (On the way out, I liberated a couple of teensy lollipops as a consolation prize.) Public transportation to his job is possible on paper but involves coordinat-ing light rail and a bus schedule for a total distance of less than three miles, and late hours are problematic. Biking might work in good weather, but walking, with few sidewalks, is not safe. The other cooks at the bar, a not especially wholesome lot, often pick Billy up and take him home, which was especially wel-come in the winter. But the long-term reliability of this arrangement and the sobriety of his colleagues are questionable. I am reconsidering whether I can swing a payment for a car that I can get into and out of with-out ten minutes of mentally winding up to it.

So, things are good. But everything hangs on a thread that could unravel at any moment. He will need luck on his side.

In other news, after dating all through junior high and high school, as my classmates predicted, Teddy Manfredi and Lisa Thomaselli were married in 1973 and today have a brood of grandchildren.

Evidently Lisa had no trouble remembering her wedding veil.

Gino is now going through his third divorce and is threatening to move back in with my mother at the tender age of sixty. Serves her right.

I'm sorry to say that Derek, the kid my horrified cousin Donna watched sliding down the wall courtesy of Sister Alberta, did not turn out okay. Related to the incident or not, he unfortunately became an addict, and things did not end well. Whether the good Sister had intuited his fate and tried in vain to beat sense into him or her brutality had just kicked him further down the path he was inevitably on, we will never know.

Gemma, my early crush, liked me "as a friend," a compliment or devastating insult depending on the context, but once past that, I got a taste of the girls' perspective from my friend. Young nuns had confided in her. One had been a Rockette—I kid you not. Look it up if you are young and never understood why audiences applaud when dancers on stage raise their legs in unison. A real Rockette! She had reddish hair and was beautiful, Gemma said—you could tell even with the "Frankenstein costume." (There was no equivalent to Sister Cecilia in any class I was in, I can assure you. I would not have forgotten.) Her parents, horrified by her career choice, had forced her to enter the convent on the threat they would disown her. She had rebelled and left to marry, having last been spotted at a football game, wearing a tank top and shorts and chasing a toddler. Another petite young nun, who couldn't have registered three digits on the scale, Sister Mary Ellen, left to marry Lonnie Dibble, the older brother of a student in my class. So, the inmates were not the only ones who wanted to escape. Sometimes the guards did too.

My cousins and I remain close, on both my father's and my mother's sides. There is nobody I would rather spend time with, even if some of it is spent arguing with them about their misguided views that do not coincide with my own.

My incredible sons, with their wonderful partners, are raising beautiful families, in homes filled with love and affection. They adore and cherish their amazing children.

THE END

Afterword

No stranger to childhood tragedy himself, at age four, A. J. and his younger brother, Jim, lost their mother, and before that, their older sister, Judy. Like many families, tragedies of all sorts have permeated through the branches of their family tree, leaving visible and invisible marks; they are rarely discussed but never, ever forgotten.

A. J.'s spirit soared above significant health issues for many years; his attention was on the things (theater, books, writing, television shows, crosswords) and the many people he loved. It was almost like the health issues were happening to someone else. He once asked, while filling out a form, what he should check for overall health: Excellent, Very Good, Good, Fair, or Poor. He was on the heart transplant list at the time.

Theater was a great passion, and for years he reviewed local community theater and previewed high school spring musicals with deep appreciation and respect. Sitting in the audience in the dark, A. J. would give himself over entirely to the production, willing to go wherever it took him, whether Broadway stars or local kids were on stage. His big, booming laugh, ringing out as an early bit of tentative comedy unfolded on stage, helped assure actors and audiences alike of a successful evening.

After aging off the transplant list, even a heart-assist device and increasingly demanding regimens failed to dampen his interest in others. His indignation could rise to fever pitch if a loved one felt slighted by someone in their lives. He worried deeply about everyone's problems, large and small, and he was always ready to laugh or make all of us laugh, to immerse himself in a story, to enjoy good food and conversation. Instead of shrinking his world, he grew it, throwing himself into fiction for the first time with this book, awakening an authentic voice, and telling a story he couldn't wait to share with readers.

Outspoken, known to poke fun, affectionate, and fiercely loving, A. J. adored his family and extended family: brother Jim, former wife Beth, nieces Sara, Jenny, Annie, Katelyn, and nephew Bub (James); in-laws; uncles and aunts; nieces and nephews by marriage; cousins on both sides; exchange students, dear friends, and some special doctors and nurses who had his back until the end. Each had an irreplaceable piece of his heart.

Like the narrator of this book, A. J.'s proudest accomplishments are his truly remarkable sons, Stephen and Scott (Sonny), and grandchildren, Marley, Amelia, Gianni, and Stella, whose boundless hearts, brains, and talents make this planet a better place every day. He lives on in them, and in this work.

Acknowledgments

The contributions of many were instrumental in the completion of this book, and I am infinitely thankful to them all for inspiration, stories and support. Deep gratitude to the supremely talented Gareth Southwell and Sidney Wuenschell for bringing A. J.'s themes and characters to life, and to Joe Pierson for his kindly red pen. Eternal love and thanks to Bettina Trautmann, for her unwavering love and support through the darkest days, and for helping bringing this book to fruition; to Bob Emmet and Connie Armstrong, for their love and generosity in helping produce this book; to John Hayes, who gave A. J. his writing start; to Joyce Reinoso, Jerry Jeannett, and Art Sample for memories and ideas; to Jim Caliendo for period detail; to Jillian Maynard Caliendo, for her priceless wedding-soup sticky notes; to Lisa Jeannett Lackey for the photograph that answered so very many questions; and to Mimi Verno, for her reminiscences and support. Mimi's wisdom and kindness helped me pursue the completion of this

book, and always came at just the right time, in just
the right words.

Elisabeth Caliendo

The author as an Altar Boy

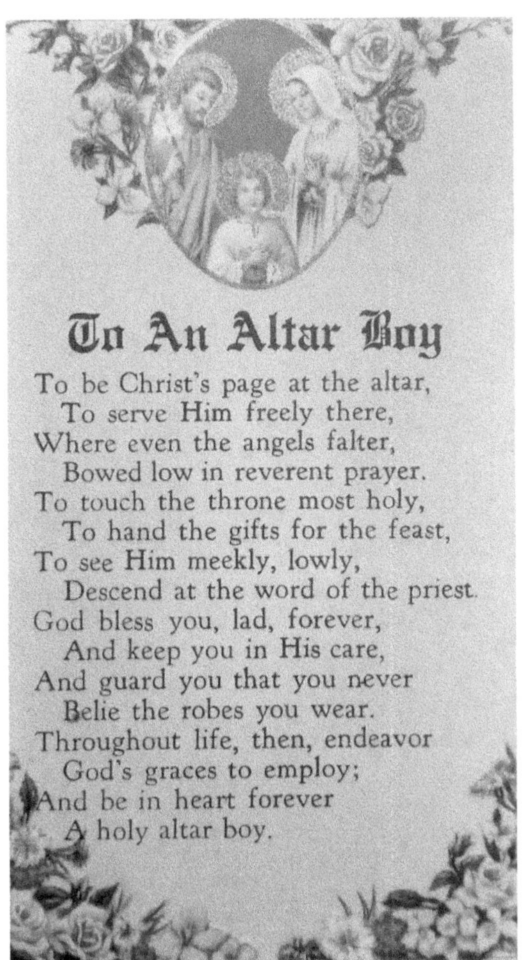

Altar Boy Prayer Card

9 798991 213905